Aminah goes to the Aquarium!

By Aminah Preston

DEDICATION

"I wrote this book for everyone that needs to read and have books."

-Aminah Preston

ACKNOWLEDGMENTS
I want to acknowledge Aaliyah, Avontae, and Laniah "La La". Happy Birthday to everyone!

One day when I was in my room, I started to think about the Aquarium.

So I called my cousins on the phone.
"Do you want to come to the Aquarium with me?"
"Yes."
"Yes."
"Yes."

All my cousins said "Yes", so we took the bus.
The bus ride was great; we saw a lot of people.

Once we arrived, we touched seaweed.

We saw a Goldfish.

We watched Squid and Jellyfish swim around.

An Octopus got scared and inked everywhere.

Baby Turtles hatched out of their shells.

Tuna swam in schools.

On our way home, my cousins and I talked about the goldfish and the baby turtles the most.

My favorite sea animal was the goldfishes.

I like the way they swim, make bubbles, and play.

When I got home I asked my Mom and Dad for a goldfish.

It took them awhile…
But they finally said "Yes"!

When I got my gold fish. I named her Little Minah.

Special Art by Eason Preston

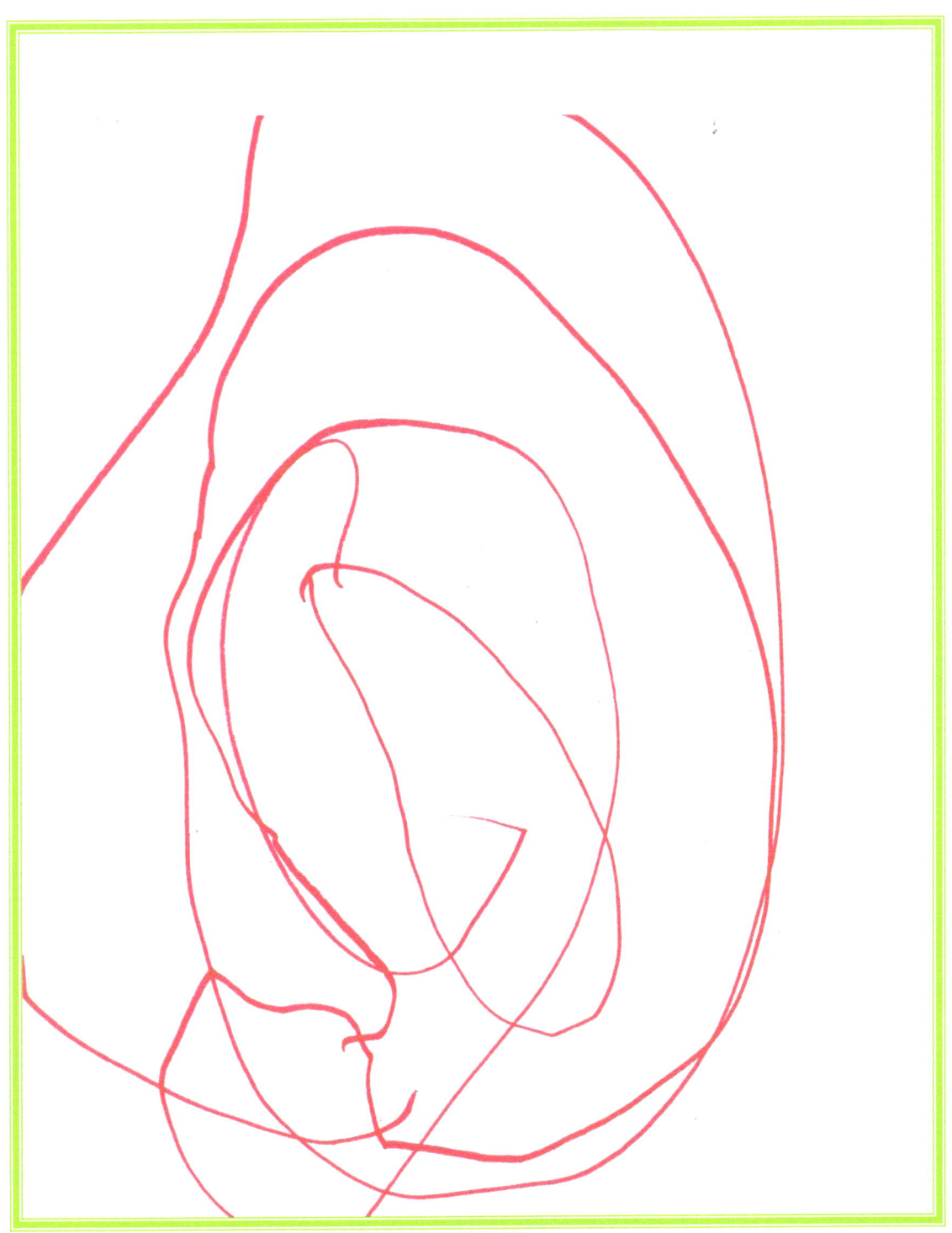

"My Tummy"

"Purple Fishy"

www.ingramcontent.com/pod-product-compliance
Lightning Source LLC
Chambersburg PA
CBHW060819290526
45792CB00005BB/1724